Camouflage Uniforms of Asian and Middle Eastern Armies

Camouflage Uniforms
of Asian and Middle Eastern Armies

J.F. Borsarello and Werner Palinckx

Schiffer Military History
Atglen, PA

Book Design by Ian Robertson.

Library of Congress Control Number: 2003114189

Printed in China.
ISBN: 0-7643-1922-1

For the largest selection of fine reference books on this and related subjects, please visit our website - **www.schifferbooks.com** - or call for a free catalog.

We are interested in hearing from authors with book ideas on related topics.

Published by Schiffer Publishing Ltd.
4880 Lower Valley Road
Atglen, PA 19310
Phone: (610) 593-1777
FAX: (610) 593-2002
E-mail: Info@schifferbooks.com.
Visit our web site at: www.schifferbooks.com
Please write for a free catalog.
This book may be purchased from the publisher.
Please include $3.95 postage.
Try your bookstore first.

In Europe, Schiffer books are distributed by:
Bushwood Books
6 Marksbury Avenue
Kew Gardens
Surrey TW9 4JF
England
Phone: 44 (0) 20 8392-8585
FAX: 44 (0) 20 8392-9876
E-mail: info@bushwoodbooks.co.uk.
Free postage in the UK. Europe: air mail at cost.
Try your bookstore first.

Contents

Foreword

Until 1945 the Asian and Middle East countries were not very interested in equipping their armies with camouflaged clothing. In fact they did not even bother creating separate uniforms and insignia for their troops, so they just used the grades and insignias of the occupying forces (Russia, England) and reintroduced them within their armed forces. Only China and Japan developed new military grades and uniforms.

Only when the vast majority of these countries gained their independence, their governments decided to create a new army structure with new uniforms and military grades. Some nations equipped their soldiers with camouflaged clothing that had proven its effectiveness during World War II.

In the beginning, these nations took over the military grades and insignia of the former occupying forces. But gradually they created more specific uniforms and special insignias that replaced the outdated equipment. This especially was the case in the Middle Eastern countries.

The crown of the British empire disappeared on many insignia in favor of the local coat of arms, the British "pip" rank insignia were often transformed into stars, and – most of all – the western camouflage patterns were adapted to the different topographical and natural conditions of Asian countries.

In the beginning of the nineties, just after the Gulf War, the camouflage patterns suffered from an inflation and were degraded to a common fashion feature. Many youngsters began to dress in camouflage clothing, and numerous non-military garments had a camouflage pattern printed to them (e.g. bathing suits, T-shirts, skirts), often in very fantasy-like camouflage patterns!

Today, this fashion continues and even extends back to the military! More and more manufacturers are developing new varieties of camouflage patterns: desert patterns; snow patterns; rocky patterns; jungle fatigues; and urban camouflage. Inspired by the many conflicts in urban regions, such as Israel and Lebanon, a gray or blue pattern emerged from the design tables.

Now, most countries want to have their own specific camouflage design so that by looking at the pattern alone, one can distinguish the country it originated from. No bother looking at the rank insignia, which – in most cases – are made of low-visibility colors, to see whom one is confronted with.

In Asia, both large and small countries all wanted to equip their armies with camouflage uniforms, which were adapted to the specific color schemes and features of that particular region they were used in. That is why at the moment these 45 countries use over 200 different camouflage patterns. Even the smallest states like Brunei, Singapore, Kuwait, and Bahrain have their own patterns.

Note: In the captions for the images, RR stands for "Reserved Rights" and AC stands for "Authors' Collection."

Acknowledgments

French embassies defense attachés and foreign embassies in Paris

Colonel B.Binnendijk of Israel
Colonel Choi Ho Gul attaché of Korea
Colonel Deregnaucourt Indonesia
Liaison officer Malcolm Chung of Singapore in Paris
Colonel Groult Philippines
Lenor Gillet Singapore embassy Paris
Corv.Captain Piat Durozoi
Colonel Protar of Vietnam
Colonel F Torres China
Commander E. Tripnaux

Collectors and collaborators

Mr. Charbonnier publisher of Militaria Magazine Paris
Mr. Czochorowski Poland
Mr. Yves Debay reporter/photographer Paris
Mr. G. Gorokhoff Paris
Mr. R. Holzel Germany
Mr. B. Jamin
Mr. Leo Karlin World militaria store Texas USA
Mr. M. Landry collector
Mr. E. Micheletti publisher of Raids Magazine Paris
Mr. Andrew Mollo collector / author
Mr. J. Nowak Poland
Mr. N.Peucelle Croatia
Mr. Y. Plasseraud collector
Mr. G.L. Plotkin publisher "Sergeant magazine" Moscow
Mr. Rutkiewicz Poland
Mr. F. Steff (+) collector
Mr. W.M. Thornton England collector / author
Mr. C.Bollaert
Mrs. M.Palinckx
Mr. Henrik Clausen Denmark
Mr. P. Courcelle Belgium
Mr. J. De Frahan France
Mr. Philip Co Philippines

BANGLADESH . BRUNEI . CAMBODIA . CHINA
INDIA . INDONESIA . JAPAN. NORTH KOREA
SOUTH KOREA . LAOS . MALAYSIA . MYANMAR

NEPAL
PHILIPPINNES
SINGAPORE
SRILANKA
TAIWAN
THAILAND
SOUTH VIETNAM
NORTHVIETNAM

1

Eastern and Southern Asia

Bangladesh

The Bangladesh army has two different camouflage patterns: the 1972 and 1990 patterns.

The drawing is very characteristic to this country; the 1990 pattern resembles the U.S. tigerstripe patterns, but with different colors on a clear background.

NCOs wear chevrons; WOs wear "pips" and one bar (red and yellow).
Junior officers wear "pips" similar to the ones used by the British army.
Senior officers have a lotus flower added to these pips.
Generals wear crossed swords with pips and the lotus flower.

Bangladesh suit 1971-1989. AC

1990 Bangladesh pattern courtesy "World militaria, Leo Karlin USA Texas."

President and officers. RR

Rank badges of Bangladesh army.

Brunei

The Brunei army is generally equipped with British camouflage patterns.

NCOs wear chevrons similar to the British ones.
WOs wear a badge with the coat of arms of Brunei.
Junior officers wear 1 to 3 pips on the shoulder boards.
Senior officers have a crown added to the shoulder boards.
Generals wear a special crown insignia with an Islamic crescent and pips.

The Brunei army was wearing British camouflage in 1990.

Rank badges of Brunei army.

British pattern courtesy "JH de Frahan Revue Defense 2000."

Cambodia

The Cambodian army wears many different camouflage suits.

Since the end of the terrible revolution in Cambodia, the newly erected army wore British DPM and U.S. woodland patterns. Some of these uniforms were made in Thailand, others in Taiwan.

Several units stationed around Angkor wore the Vietnamese 1970 Tigerstripe model.

It is curious to note that the Cambodian army is wearing badges of the French army.

NCOs wear a type of British chevrons in gold ornated with a Cambodian symbol.

WOs wear a silver bar

Junior officers wear 1 to 3 golden bars.

Senior officers wear 4 to 5 golden bars.

Generals wear golden bars with a well-decorated foliage bar underneath.

Cap badges were modified in 1998

Cambodian generals wearing two types of camouflage patterns: the British pattern and – in the back – a duck hunter pattern, courtesy "JH de Frahan Revue Defense 2000."

Sort of U.S. 1981 woodland camo with different colors, courtesy "JH de Frahan Revue Defense 2000." RR

Duck hunter pattern.

Cambodian generals with a French diplomat courtesy "JH de Frahan Revue Defense 2000."

Cambodian soldier with patterns made in Thailand courtesy "JH de Frahan Revue Defense 2000."

Cambodian cap badges A & B are former symbols of communist inspiration. All others are present time symbols.

Above: *Rank badges of the Cambodian army, similar to the French insignia.*

Cambodian unit badges: paratroopers, commando, and Special Forces. The badge with skull, anchor, sword, and wings is of Indonesian origin. Cambodian commandos have been trained in Indonesia.

China

It was only in 1975 that the world found out that the Chinese army had adopted camouflage patterns. In this year the Chinese published the first photos of Chinese soldiers in camouflage uniforms. The first pattern was brown with small dark brown spots. This pattern was used on a heavy padded winter suit.

Later a wide variety of patterns were developed, most of them very different from the already existing patterns in other countries. This made the patterns difficult to compare and describe.

In 1980 the "little spot pattern" emerged; this was very similar to the South Korean pattern. Also, in 1980 they created a sort of U.S. woodland pattern and used it for padded winter suits.

After 1981 the patterns more and more looked like the U.S. woodland pattern.

In 1990 a new wave of patterns colored the Chinese uniforms. Every army branch had its own specific camo pattern. One wonders if the border guards have a very distinct camouflage design?

The woodland pattern used by the infantry looked very similar to the U.S. M65 or M81 Woodland patterns.

Since 1990 the marines are wearing a nice white-blue-black pattern, whereas the Special Forces and mountain troops are wearing a white uniform spotted with black drawings representing dead tree branches – very effective camo design.

The last pattern seen in 2000 worn by South Chinese forces consists of a brown background with small dark green drawings covered with white and black spots.

The rank badges of the Chinese army were based on the old Russian insignia. This lasted until the 1990s.

NCOs are now wearing rank chevrons.

With ten ranks of NCOs and WOs, the Chinese army has really modified its uniforms. In 1959 there were only 5 ranks in these categories.

The heavy gold embroidered shoulder boards for the parade dress have been modified to fit the lighter summer uniforms and battle dresses.

Officers and generals wear single black (army) or blue (air force) shoulder boards with bars, stars, and stripes.

"Little spots" side of the first Chinese camo, seen in Mongolia.

The other side of the uniform at left, Mongolia 1980.

Above: *The 2nd camo worn by an infantry soldier 1980. RR*
Above left: *The 2nd camo also seen in 1980 for infantry, reversible with little spots, light material. RR*

Variant of little spots pattern, green background.

Good view of the 2 reversible suits " little spots" in Mongolia. RR

Borderguards 1990 courtesy "World militaria, Leo Karlin USA Texas."

Winter padded camo uniform 1985 similar to U.S. M81 woodland. AC

The Special Forces pattern courtesy "World militaria, Leo Karlin USA Texas."

Infantry in woodland pattern courtesy "PLA life 2002" courtesy of military attaché of the embassy of France, Beijing.

NCOs of the Chinese marines wearing the old version of rank insignia in 2000 courtesy "PLA life 2000."

Mountain troops pattern courtesy " PLA life 2000."

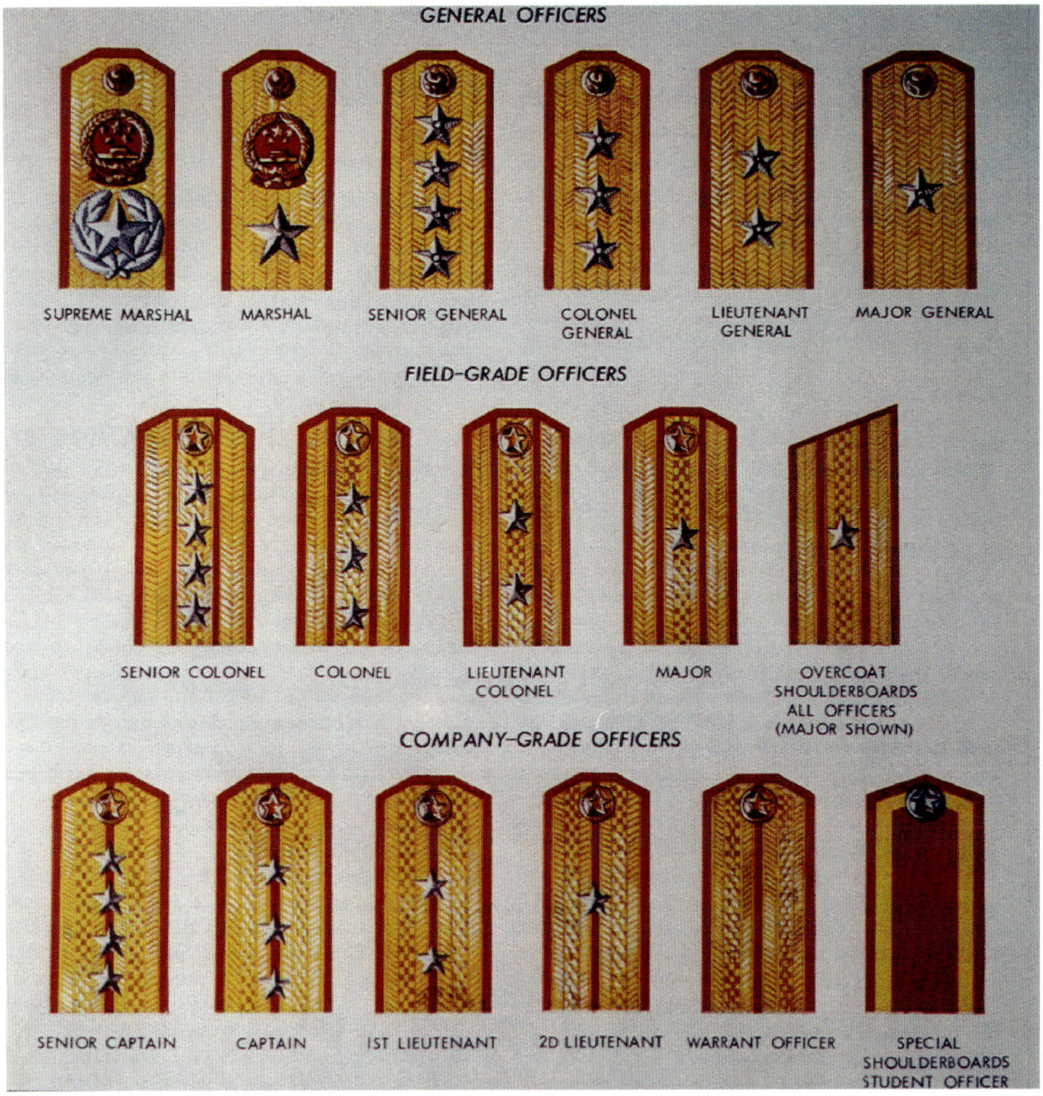

GENERAL OFFICERS

SUPREME MARSHAL
MARSHAL
SENIOR GENERAL
COLONEL GENERAL
LIEUTENANT GENERAL
MAJOR GENERAL

FIELD-GRADE OFFICERS

SENIOR COLONEL
COLONEL
LIEUTENANT COLONEL
MAJOR
OVERCOAT SHOULDERBOARDS ALL OFFICERS (MAJOR SHOWN)

COMPANY-GRADE OFFICERS

SENIOR CAPTAIN
CAPTAIN
IST LIEUTENANT
2D LIEUTENANT
WARRANT OFFICER
SPECIAL SHOULDERBOARDS STUDENT OFFICER

The first 1959 rank badges plate courtesy "Pamphlet 30-55 HQ depot of U.S. army, Washington, DC 29/x/59."

New rank badges of Chinese NCOs and WOs 2001.

Simplified rank insignia on the battle dress, here a colonel and a corporal courtesy "World militaria, Leo Karlin USA Texas."

Air Forces lieutenant colonel with blue shoulder boards. RR

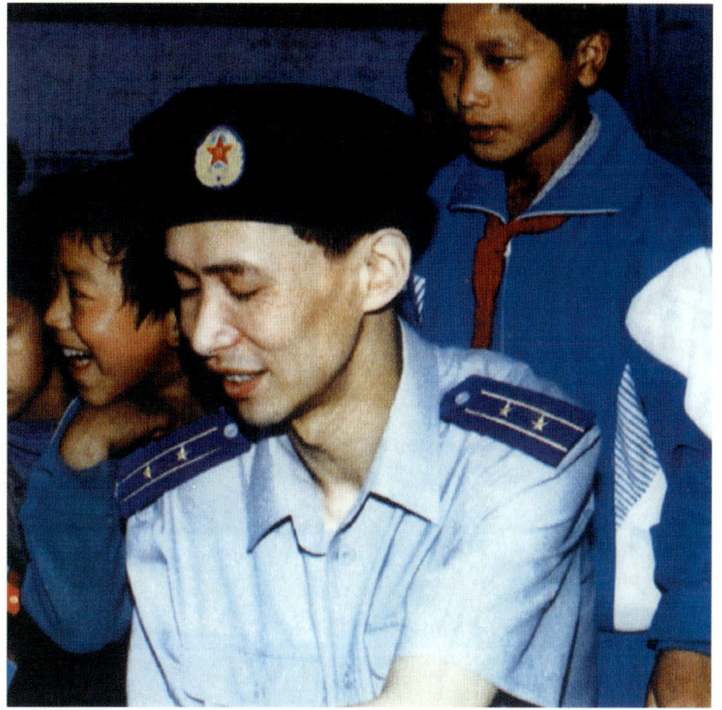

The shoulder boards of generals have also been simplified for light and summer uniforms. RR

India

The first camouflage jacket used by the Indian army was very similar to the British Denison smock. Today this pattern is outdated, however, the photo of an overall for helicopter pilots shows that this pattern still exists for certain garments.

Paratroopers wore this pattern until 1975.

After 1980, a new pattern appeared, it had ragged leaves with green and brown colors.

The rank insignia are similar to British insignia:

Chevrons for NCOs.

Officers are wearing stars instead of pips and the British crown has been replaced by the three lions of India.

Paratroopers in 1978 with old pattern camouflage. RR

First Indian pattern for paratroopers. AC

Overall for helicopter pilots. AC

The new camouflage of the Indian army. AC

Indian soldiers of IFOR in former Yugoslavia wearing the new pattern. RR

Plate with ranks for officers.

Indonesia

The Indonesian army has a wide variety of camouflage uniforms. From 1960 till today no less than 10 different patterns occurred.

The first three patterns appeared in 1960; the design was similar to the U.S. "Kingkard"patterns. One pattern had vineyard leaves in its design. It was only at the end of 1961 that the Indonesians developed their own patterns: long vertical waves with a very good camouflage effect in the jungle. Most of the jungle vegetation is vertical, though further on it proved to be effective in savanna and forest environments.

In 1970 a curious splinter pattern for air forces with pink, brown, green, and yellow splinters was developed.

In 1980 another pattern appeared; it had long waves but they were tighter, further on the design had vertical drawings with dominant green and blue colors.

A third type of the long waves pattern uniforms, with long vertical stripes, was distributed to the paratroopers in 1980. The colors were dark green and dark blue on a yellow green background.

Recently a last type of camouflage emerged in Afghanistan. It has the typical Indonesian design and was worn by the troops of Massoud in 2001. The pattern has a clear background covered with large green and black spots with ragged sides. A sort-like camo pattern can be seen worn by the commandos of Mohammed Abror (commando Muhammadiyah), which was first published in the French magazine "Le Point" in 1988.

The rank insignia are particular for Indonesia:
NCOs wear chevrons
WOs wear broken lines
Junior officers wear 1 to 3 golden bars
Senior officers wear 1 to 3 flowers
Generals wear stars

These ranks were modified in 2002; all shoulder boards show the TNI initials (Indonesian National Army). Senior officers wear the Garuda eagle instead of the flowers (3 Garuda = colonel).

Junior officers are still wearing bars, but now they are joined bars.
NCOs wear gold chevrons, corporals red chevrons, and troops 1 to 3 red bars.
All ranks wear their unit patches, mostly in red, on the upper arm.
Parade uniforms have golden shoulder boards.

1960 pattern very similar to the U.S. "Kingkard" 1943 pattern courtesy "World militaria, Leo Karlin USA Texas."

1960 U.S. vineyard leaves pattern used in 1950 during the Korean war and later copied by Thailand, courtesy "World militaria, Leo Karlin USA Texas."

1960 typical Indonesian pattern with long waves. AC

Above: *The pink background splinters for paratroopers courtesy "World militaria, Leo Karlin USA Texas."* Above left: *An Indonesian general wearing the long waves pattern at present time. Booklet of Indonesian army courtesy of military attaché of France in Indonesia.* Left: *The 1980 new long vertical waves.* Below: *Another pattern showing long vertical waves, dark blue and dark green colors courtesy "World militaria, Leo Karlin USA Texas."*

The Indonesian 1980 pattern for marines, or a very similar one, seen in Afghanistan, courtesy "World militaria, Leo Karlin USA Texas."

The British DPM was also used in the Indonesian army.

Above: *Rank badges and cap badge of officers of the Indonesian army in 2000.* Left: *The camouflage of the Muhammadiyah commandos. RR*

Above left: *Rank badges of generals, WOs, and NCOs in 2000.* Left: *The new ranks of the Indonesian army in 2002.* Above right: *Arm patches for the various units.*

Left: *Army generals and navy admirals of Indonesia ECPA.* Right: *Army general and air force general of Indonesia.*

Japan

The Japanese army only adapted 2 camouflage uniforms. The first pattern was used from 1980 on and consisted of spots in three colors – brown, green, and black – on a clear background. All units used this pattern.

In 1995 a second pattern was introduced. This was very similar to the German 1976 Marquardt and Schulz pattern, which has since then been used by all German troops. It is made of a mixture of tiny spots in brown, green, and black and is very effective in woodlands.

Because of the efficacy of this pattern many countries, including Canada and the U.S., where it is used for the marines, adopted it.

After WWII and later on in the sixties Japan was not allowed to have an army of its own, so they created the JSDF (Japanese self-defense Forces). The rank insignia differed completely from that used in the Imperial army:

Soldiers and NCOs use chevrons.
WOs have special collar tabs
Officers have flowers with bars
Generals use 1 to 4 flowers

Japanese armored crew member in 1980 camo pattern. RR JSDF

Close up view of Japanese 1980 pattern, courtesy "Wild Mook-Uniforms and equipment of the JSDF World Photo Press."

The new Japanese pattern, courtesy "Wild Mook-Uniforms and equipment of the JSDF, World Photo Press."

Japanese soldiers in camouflage uniforms at rest for dinner, courtesy "Wild Mook-Uniforms and equipment of the JSDF, World Photo Press."

Close up view of the new Japanese pattern courtesy "Wild Mook-Uniforms and equipment of the JSDF World Photo Press."

Rank badges of the Japanese army: 1st line NCOs; 2nd line Wos; 3rd line officers and a general.

1st line WOs, 2nd line NCOs. RR

Cap badges: air force and (below) army.

Left: *A Japanese air force general, courtesy "Wild Mook-Uniforms and equipment of the JSDF, World Photo Press."*

Some unit badges of the army and air force.

North Korea

It was very difficult to obtain any recent information about the camouflage and ranks used in the North Korean army. The authors only encountered information about 1950-1960 materials, mostly of Russian origin.

After 1970 most existing camo patterns were abandoned and replaced by a pattern with clear gray background and large green and brown oak leaves. Unfortunately, only one bad picture of this pattern was discovered.

Rank insignia were based upon the Russian insignia from the 1950s:

They had 5 ranks for NCOs and WOs, now the same insignia still exist but two new ones have been added.

The piping is blue for air force, red for army, and green for border troops.

Specialty insignia worn on the collar tabs are similar to the Russian ones.

Russian pattern for snipers 1942. AC

Camouflage uniforms of North Korea photo handbook 1960 U.S. HQ Washington, DC.

Russian pattern 1960 for North Korea. RR

Close up view of 1960 pattern.

Present time camouflage in a bad photo. RR

Drawing showing very approximately the 2000 North Korean pattern.

Three NCOs and WO of the North Korean army. RR

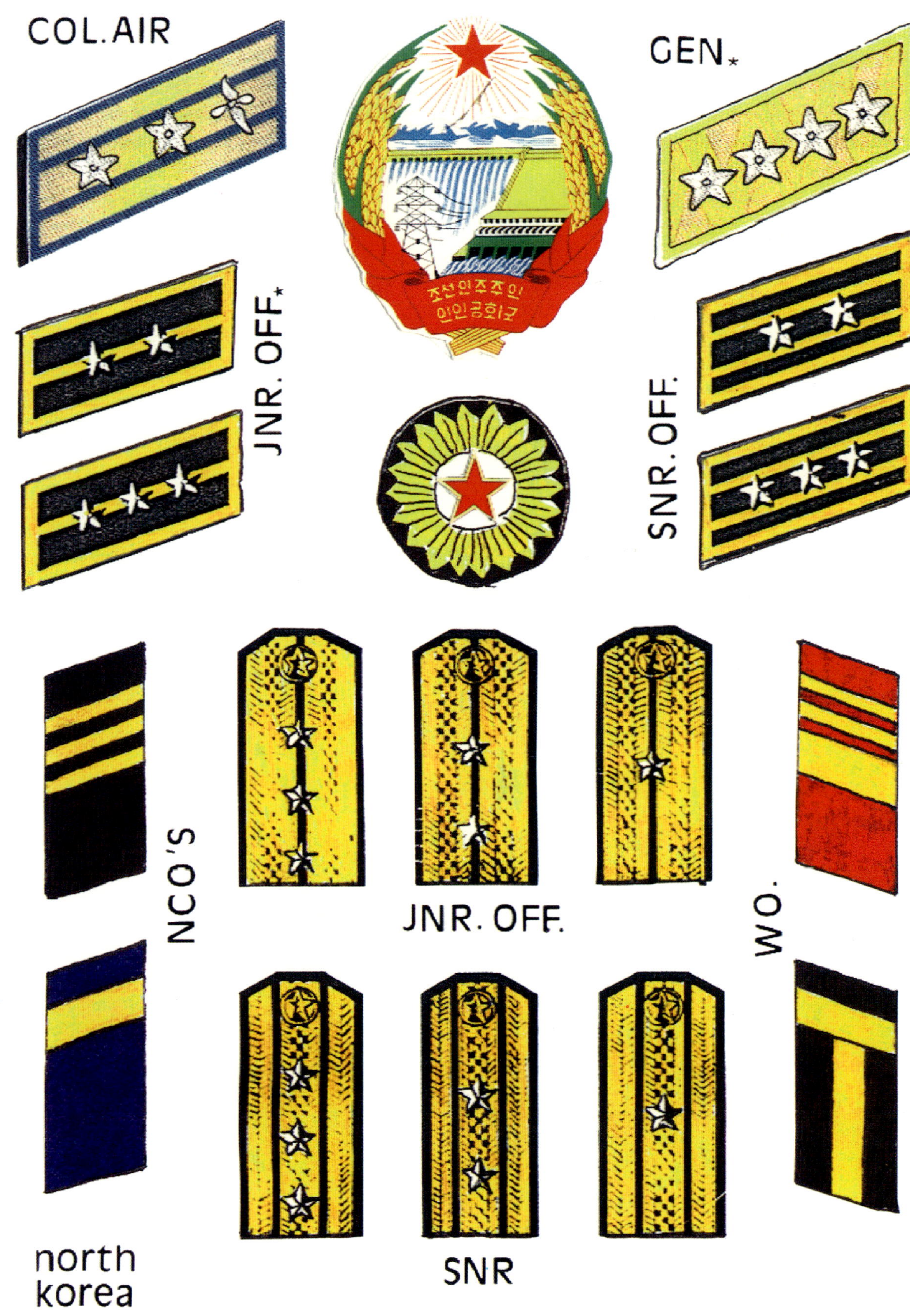

New 2001 rank insignia table.

A sergeant with North Korean soldiers. RR

1960 South Korean patterns. AC

South Korea

Together with Indonesia, the South Korean army uses the most camouflage patterns. No less than 14 different camouflage patterns have been used between 1960 and today. The country has sold its camouflage to Chili, Palestine, Afghanistan, Guatemala, Peru, and several Central American countries.

After the Korean War, the South Korean army has repeatedly manufactured the U.S. army 1944 duck hunter pattern, but with different colors. This resulted in new patterns with jigsaw puzzle drawings, splinters, and later on U.S. M65 woodland designs.

Students in schools for future military professions now wear a special uniform similar to the military camouflage uniforms.

The rank insignia have been changed four times since 1950:
Now soldier and corporals wear bars
NCOs wear chevrons and a S.Korean symbol
Officers wear flowers and a S.Korean symbol
Generals wear stars and the symbol

Today the South Korean army, together with the Japanese army, is one of the most modern and well-equipped armies of Asia.

1960 South Korean pattern.

1960 South Korean pattern, courtesy "World militaria, Leo Karlin USA Texas."

1960 South Korean pattern, courtesy "World militaria, Leo Karlin USA Texas."

1970 South Korean pattern, courtesy "World militaria, Leo Karlin USA Texas."

1970-1980 South Korean marine pattern, courtesy "World militaria, Leo Karlin USA Texas."

1970-1980 South Korean tanker pattern. RR

Close up of the 1970 pattern, courtesy "World militaria, Leo Karlin USA Texas."

Above: *Close up view of South Korean instructors' pattern.* Left: *Pattern for South Korean instructors.*

South Korean 1970 pattern for navy commandos, courtesy "Wild Mook-Uniforms and equipment of the JSDF, World Photo Press."

South Korean 1970 pattern for navy commandos, courtesy "Wild Mook-Uniforms and equipment of the JSDF, World Photo Press."

Above: *1990 South Korean woodland pattern, courtesy "World militaria, Leo Karlin USA Texas."* Left: *1990 South Korean woodland pattern, courtesy "World militaria, Leo Karlin USA Texas."*

South Korean general's parade uniform ECPA.

Left: *This South Korean pattern was used in Vietnam.*

South Korean general's parade uniform ECPA.

This pattern is not a military camouflage! It is made for students at military schools who have not graduated yet.

Military ranks table. RR

Laos

The Laotian army has long been wearing Thai camouflage patterns. Today they have chosen a special leaf pattern made in Thailand based upon the U.S. M65 camouflage. It has a clear green background and dark brown and yellow drawings.

The rank insignia are special and differ a lot from the ones used in neighboring countries:

Corporals wear chevrons in white or red.
NCOs wear 1 to 3 chevrons
WOs a silver or golden bar
Junior officers wear stars without golden edge
Senior officers wear stars and a sun and have golden edged shoulder boards.
All backgrounds of the shoulder boards are red. A khaki back ground is used for battle dress shoulder boards.
Generals wear embroidered shoulder boards with stars.
The cap badge always has a sun, foliage and Asian mythological images.

Variant of the Laotian camouflage pattern courtesy "World militaria, Leo Karlin USA Texas."

Laotian pattern of Thai origin.

Close up of a general's shoulder board, M. Landry collection.

Laotian soldiers in camouflage uniforms.

Cap badges and insignia of the Laotian army, courtesy M. Landry collection.

Rank insignia of the Laotian army, courtesy M. Landry collection.

Malaysia

The Malaysian army has three major camouflage patterns. The first pattern was specially designed for Malaysia. The two other patterns are of Thai origin.

The rank insignia were very similar to the British insignia, but they were modified in 2002. A national badge in a circle has replaced the stars. The crown used by the British was joined with an Islamic crescent and star.

Present time camo with ragged bush. AC

Close up of ragged bush pattern. AC

The second pattern of the Malaysian army: mixed tiger stripes and woodland camo, courtesy "World militaria, Leo Karlin USA Texas."

The 3rd camouflage pattern of the Malaysian army, courtesy Yves Debay.

Rank insignia of the Malaysian army.

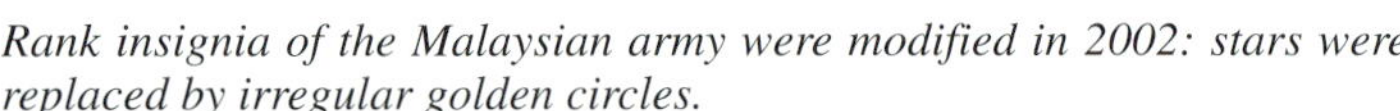

Rank insignia of the Malaysian army were modified in 2002: stars were replaced by irregular golden circles.

Myanmar (former Birma)

All units of the army of Myanmar are now wearing camouflaged uniforms of Thai origin.

In the north there was a rebel movement, the Karens rebels, who also used camouflage but without any regulation.

The ranks of the Myanmar army are very similar to the British:

Soldiers and NCOs wear chevrons

Junior officers wear Burmese stars in gold.

Senior officers wear large 8 pointed stars with 2 branches of foliage and 5 pointed stars over them.

Generals wear the same insignia, but a crown of foliage surrounds the largest star.

The word "MYANMAR" written in Burmese is placed under all badges.

The cap badge has a red background with a star, anchor and wings surrounded by golden foliage. This badge is also worn on collar tabs.

Camo pattern of the army of Myanmar, photo courtesy Y. Debay.

Camo from Thai origin worn in Myanmar, and also by the Karens rebels, courtesy "World militaria, Leo Karlin USA Texas."

Camo from Thai and Chinese origin worn by Myanmar soldiers and Karens rebels, courtesy "World militaria, Leo Karlin USA Texas."

The word MYANMAR in Burmese under each rank insignia.

General of Myanmar, courtesy Hernandez l'express magazine 2001, courtesy "World militaria, Leo Karlin USA Texas."

Generals' cap insignia Myanmar.

Rank table of the Myanmar army.

Nepal

The Nepalese army has three different camouflage patterns. The camouflage is not of foreign origin and was designed and manufactured by the Nepalese themselves.

Nepal provided the British army during WWII with the famous Gurkha soldiers, equipped with their well-known long Gurkha knives. This knife also appears on most of the cap badges and rank insignia.

First Nepalese pattern 1990, courtesy "World militaria, Leo Karlin USA Texas."

Second Nepalese pattern 1990, courtesy "World militaria, Leo Karlin USA Texas."

Ranks are generally black on a red background:

Single bars for corporals and NCOs
WOs wear a moon or sun on the sleeve
Officers wear crossed Gurkha knives with a moon and stars.
Senior officers wear knives with a sword joined by a moon or sun.
Generals wear crossed Gurkha knives, a sword and a crown surrounded by foliage as cap badge.

Close-up view of third Nepalese pattern.

Third Nepalese pattern, courtesy "Raids magazine 1999 IFOR France."

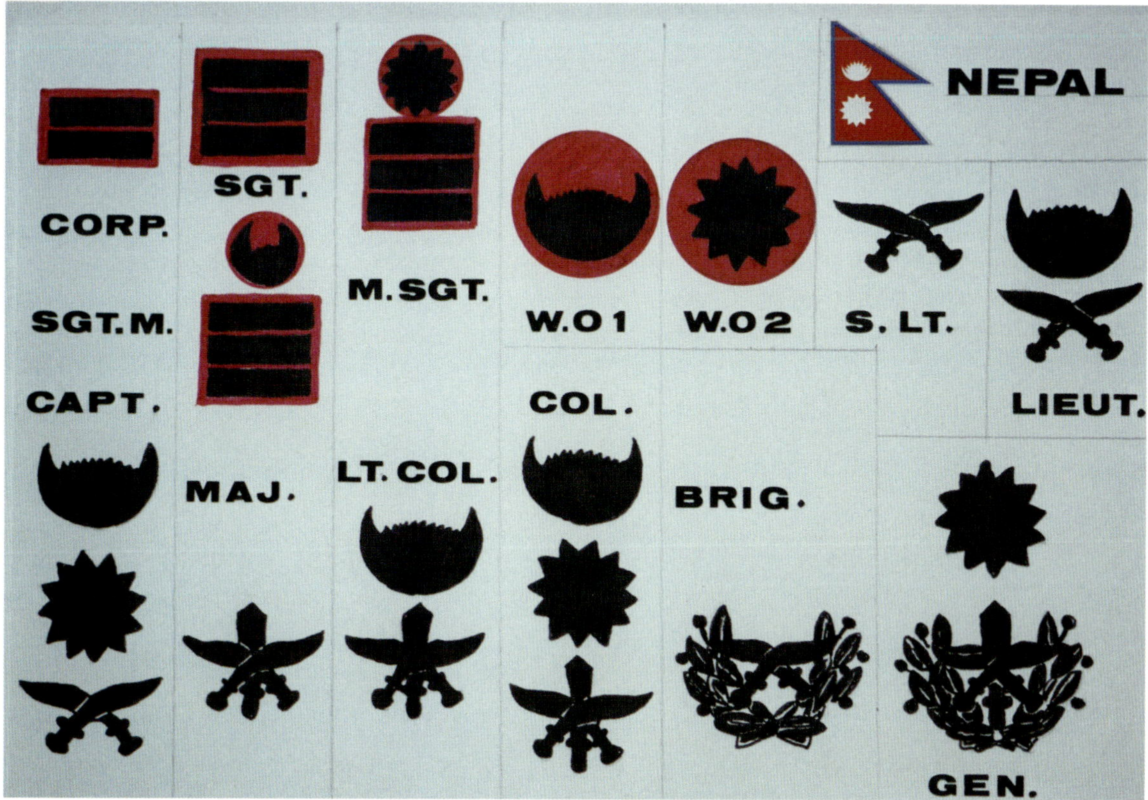

Nepalese army rank insignia.

Philippines

The army of the Philippines uses many camouflage patterns. In 1960 two different patterns emerged, which were very similar to the U.S. Kingkard pattern. These were rapidly replaced by a Philippine camouflage design that was used by both the army and rebel groups.

It consists of splinters with black, green, and brown colors, a bit like the U.S. M65 leaf pattern. Two variants of this type existed.

In 1980 two new trial versions were released. They had designs with ragged leaves, large spots, and little oval olive-like spots. This pattern was mainly used by army instructors and Special Forces. At the same time the army also started to adopt a camouflage pattern very similar to the U.S. woodland pattern with black "amoeba" drawings.

In 1990 the police used a special camo with "chocolate chips" – similar to the U.S. desert pattern – on a pinkish background covered with green and brown large spots.

In 1991 a new desert area pattern was introduced. It had ragged drawings and sand colors. This pattern was used in Arab armies around the Persian Gulf.

Further on that year a "black worms" camouflage showed up. It had black worm designs together with large blue and brown spots.

In 1995 another pattern with chocolate chips was manufactured, but this time with blue and large green drawings. This uniform was seen worn by the rebels who took European hostages on GOLO Island.

Finally, in 2001 the whole army used a woodland pattern. At a distance one only sees some clear spots; the rest of the pattern tends to fade in the background it is used in.

The rank insignia of the Philippine army have been modified recently. Rank badges are worn on the shoulder boards or on the beret over the national cap badge.

Now WOs and NCOs wear chevrons and bars. The air force's chevrons have the Philippine cockade (red, white, and blue) in the V-shape.

Junior officers wear triangles, golden for the army, silver for air forces.

Generals wear golden stars

The cap badge shows the typical triangle, an eight-pointed star with a golden circle, a crown of foliage, and three five-pointed stars, which is the coat of arms of the Philippines.

One of the first patterns of the Philippine army, courtesy collection of de Groote Brussels.

Variant of the first pattern. AC

1980 pattern used for instructors and Special Forces, courtesy "World militaria, Leo Karlin USA Texas."

A pattern with long vertical stripes, like the tigerstripe pattern with a brown background, used by rebels, courtesy "soldier of fortune magazine 55."

Close-up of previous picture, courtesy "World militaria, Leo Karlin USA Texas."

1980 pattern used for instructors and Special Forces, courtesy "World militaria, Leo Karlin USA Texas."

The black amoebae pattern, courtesy Philip Co Manila.

Police pink background pattern, courtesy "World militaria, Leo Karlin USA Texas."

Above: *Desert sand pattern of the Philippines.* Right: *Old Philippines camouflage pattern.*

Black worms pattern, courtesy de Groote Brussels.

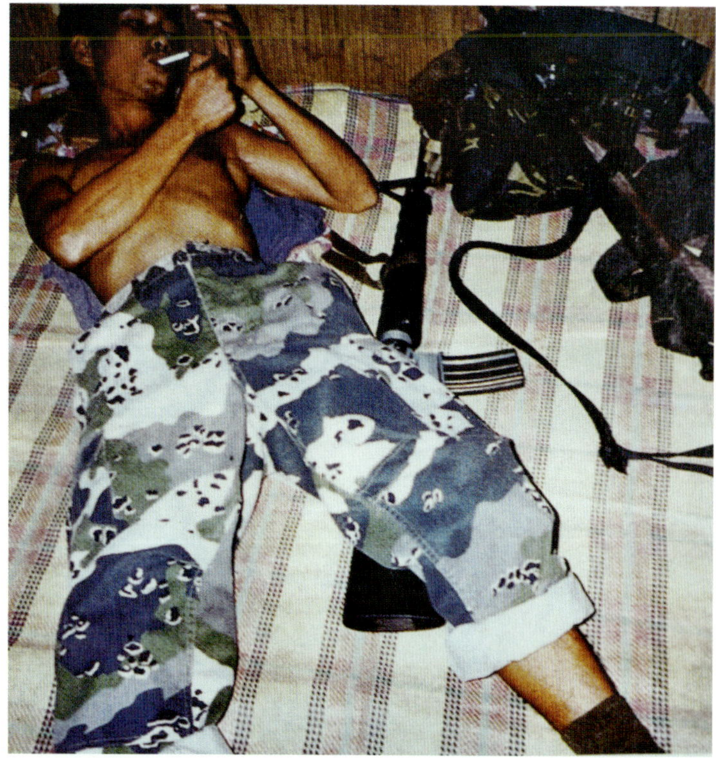

Guerilla with a variant of the pink background pattern.

*The new 2001 Philippine pattern (*another variant seen in photo at right*) courtesy of the French embassy in Manila.*

Plate with rank insignia for army and air forces. RR

The French military attaché with a Philippine general and colonel.

A senior officer of the Philippine army, courtesy Dr. Landry.

Sri Lanka

The army of Sri Lanka is wearing two different camouflage suits: the British DPM and the (Tamil) tigerstripe pattern. Tamil rebels generally wear the same camouflage patterns.

The rank insignia are as follows:
The national shield with crossed swords for generals
A shield and eight-pointed star for senior officers
1 to 3 eight-pointed stars for junior officers
A shield on the sleeve for WOs
Chevrons for NCOs

The cap badges consist of the national shield and crossed swords with an inscription for the army; the air force has a wheel and eagle in a circle.

Unit badges of the Philippines' army and cap badges.

Tamil girl with tigerstripe camouflage, courtesy "TH Charlier Raids magazine France."

Close-up view of the tigerstripe, courtesy "World militaria, Leo Karlin USA Texas."

Rank insignia plate: 1&2 cap badge for the army and air force; 3 national shield; 4 junior officers; 5 senior officers; 6 generals; and 7 NCOs.

Singapore

The small army of Singapore is very well-equipped and manufactures its own camouflage uniforms and insignia.

In 1960, the first camouflage pattern appeared with two variants: a pattern with vertical, short ragged drawings and black, green, and brown blotches; and the same design, but with different colors (dark green and pale brown on a green or khaki background).

After 1975 a new pattern emerged, similar to the U.S. M65 leaf pattern but with slightly different drawings.

In 1990 they changed the colors again, this time on a light green background.

The rank insignia are:
Golden stars for generals
1 to 3 Singapore national emblems for senior officers
1 to 3 golden bars for junior officers
WOs wear inverted 'V' chevrons with a curl and a shield (see 8 – 11 on the plate) They wear their rank on the shoulder boards.
NCOs wear chevrons (4-7 on the plate)
Corporals wear a curl with 1 or 2 chevrons in V

The new 1975 pattern.

The 1960 camouflage patterns. AC

Close-up view of the 1960 pattern.

The 1990 pattern, courtesy "World militaria, Leo Karlin USA Texas."

A soldier of Singapore in camouflage uniform, courtesy military attaché in France.

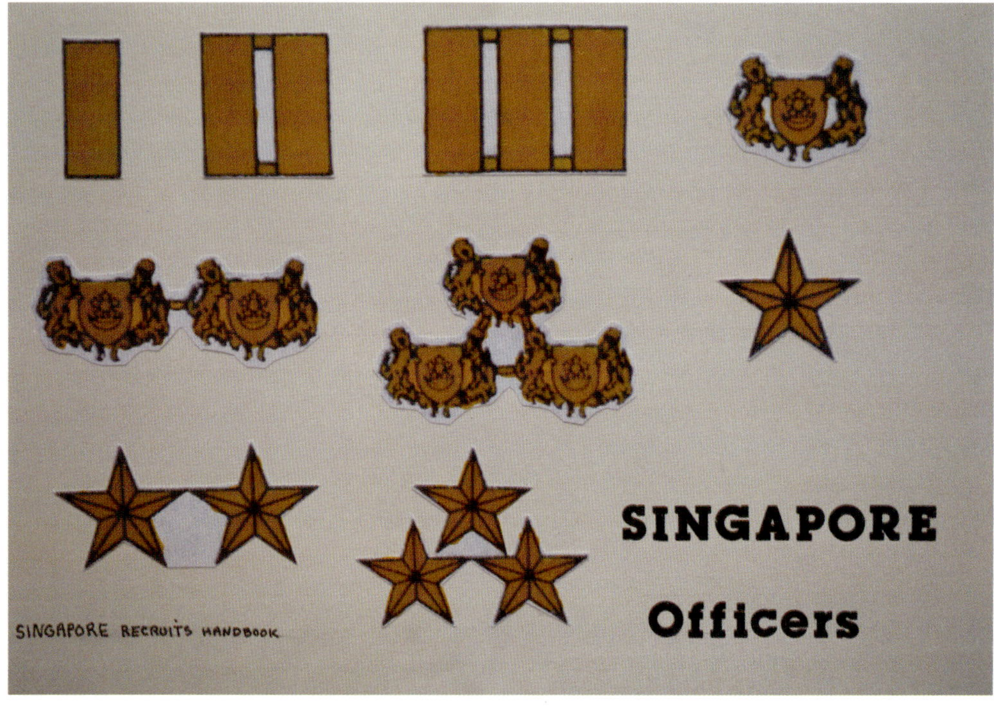

Plate with rank insignia for officers. RR

Plate with rank insignia for WOs and NCOs. RR

Taiwan

Since it was separated from China in 1949, Taiwan has developed its army into a considerable force.

The first camouflage pattern was introduced in 1978 and was based upon the U.S. tigerstripe camo pattern used during the Vietnam War. However, this Taiwanese pattern had thin white drawings, whereas the U.S. pattern has green ones. Today the Taiwanese marine forces mainly use this pattern.

In 1990 they introduced a new pattern, very similar to the U.S. M81 woodland camo, with long, yellow drawings, mainly used by paratroopers. At the same time the army developed a different pattern with mostly vertical stripes of a light green-yellow color.

The present rank insignia of the Taiwanese army differ a lot from the ones used by the nationalist forces of Chang Kai Check from 1930 to 1946:

Now generals wear golden stars
Senior officers wear 1 to 3 golden lotus flowers
Junior officers wear 1 to 3 golden bars
NCOs wear chevrons and bars (yellow for the army, silver for the air force)

The cap badge consists of a Chinese sun surrounded by foliage; joined wings replace the foliage for air force troops.

Marines wear the NCO ranks on a red background (3). Each unit has different arm badges: commandos (1); divers (2); paratroopers (4); marines (5); and paratrooper school (6).

The first pattern for marine troops.

The Taiwanese tigerstripe pattern, courtesy "World militaria, Leo Karlin USA Texas."

Taiwanese marine, courtesy Yves Debay.

1990 paratroopers pattern, similar to U.S. woodland, courtesy "World militaria, Leo Karlin USA Texas."

Close-up view of Taiwanese marine, courtesy Y. Debay.

1990 army pattern with different drawings, courtesy "World militaria, Leo Karlin USA Texas."

Insignia of the marines and other units.

Rank badges of the Taiwanese army. AC

Thailand

Thailand is the third biggest manufacturer of camouflage clothing in Asia. Many armies in the world used camouflage of Thai origin during the eighties and nineties of last century.

In the beginning they mainly copied U.S. patterns that were used in the Vietnam War, such as the M65 and M81 woodland camo, the tigerstripe, and all possible color variants of these patterns. Later they tried to copy another U.S. camo pattern, the 1950 vineyard leaves pattern used in Korea, but this was quickly abandoned.

Many of the neighboring countries bought the Thai – made camouflage uniforms: Malaysia, Cambodia, Laos, Bangladesh, and New Guinea.

No new concept has been manufactured since the latest development in 1996, which was another variant copy of the U.S. M81 woodland camo.

The Thai rank insignia are still the same as the ones used in 1940 under the government of president Pibul San Gram, chief of the Thai (Siam) army during WWII:

Generals wear golden shoulder boards with a golden pagoda and stars.

Senior officers wear shoulder boards with a golden edge, a golden band and stars with a pagoda.

Junior officers wear golden edged shoulder boards and 1 to 3 golden stars.

WOs wear reversed chevrons 1 to 3 with one bar

NCOs wear chevrons

1970 pattern Special Forces.

1972 police pattern, courtesy "World militaria, Leo Karlin USA Texas."

1970 Thai tigerstripe, courtesy "World militaria, Leo Karlin USA Texas."

1980 Thai paratroopers, courtesy "World militaria, Leo Karlin USA Texas."

1980 Thai paratroopers, courtesy "World militaria, Leo Karlin USA Texas."

1980 typical leave pattern in two different colors.

1985 vineyard leaves pattern clear type. AC

1985 vineyard leaves pattern dark type.

1990 marines pattern, courtesy "World militaria, Leo Karlin USA Texas."

1995 Thai pattern sold all over Asia.

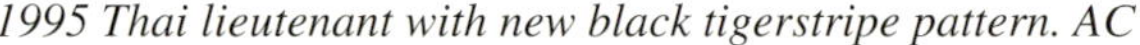

1995 Thai lieutenant with new black tigerstripe pattern. AC

1995 Thai WO with blue night camouflage. AC

Above right: *Thai officers and a French admiral.*
Right: *General of Thailand. RR*

Rank insignia and cap badges of the Thai army. AC

Vietnam

The Popular Army of Vietnam (PAVN) started to wear camouflage uniforms from 1968 on. Before that date its soldiers usually wore black or plain colored uniforms. The patterns developed by this army, involved in continuous fighting from 1948 to 1975, are all manufactured in Vietnam and have not been seen used by any other army. When opposed to French forces, the army only had olive green or black colored uniforms. Fighting the U.S. army the uniforms remained the same; only in the early seventies did camouflaged uniforms start to emerge.

In 1980 an "amoeba" pattern was used by police forces. It had green and brown spots and was designed similarly to the U.S. woodland camouflage.

In 1990 the Vietnamese developed their final camouflage pattern: ragged horizontal stripes and palms in the background.

Photographic evidence, however, shows that in 2001 the PAVN still used the older patterns, so that one can say that today the Vietnamese army uses a mixture of all the types of camouflage they ever developed.

The rank insignia of the PAVN are worn on the shoulder boards and collar tabs of the battle dress.

Generals wear golden shoulder boards with silver stars; on the battle dress they wear a golden edged red collar tab with silver stars.

Senior officers wear yellow shoulder boards with silver bars and 1 to 4 stars. For the battle dress this changes into red collar tabs with bars and stripes.

NCOs wear 1 to 3 red bars on the shoulder boards

Corporals wear chevrons, soldiers stars on the collar tabs.

1968 the first PAVN pattern was made of black or brown tears on a clear green background.

Close-up view of the 1970 second pattern.

The second type of PAVN camouflage: little spots on a dark green or clear green background.

1980 third pattern similar to woodland.

1980 the police pattern amoeba pattern, courtesy "World militaria, Leo Karlin USA Texas."

1990 the definitive new pattern, courtesy "World militaria, Leo Karlin USA Texas."

General Giap with his rank insignia on the collar tabs.

1990 close-up view of the pattern.

Present photo of the PAVN showing the variety of camouflage uniforms used, courtesy French military attaché in Vietnam.

PAVN officer, note the cap badge.

Plate with rank insignia of the PAVN, courtesy " handbook nr 30.55 Sino-Soviet ground forces Asian members HQ dept of the army Washington DC 25."

PAVN captain in battle dress, courtesy " handbook nr 30.55 Sino-Soviet ground forces Asian members HQ dept of the army Washington DC 25."

PAVN NCOs in battle dress, courtesy " handbook nr 30.55 Sino-Soviet ground forces Asian members HQ dept of the army Washington DC 25."

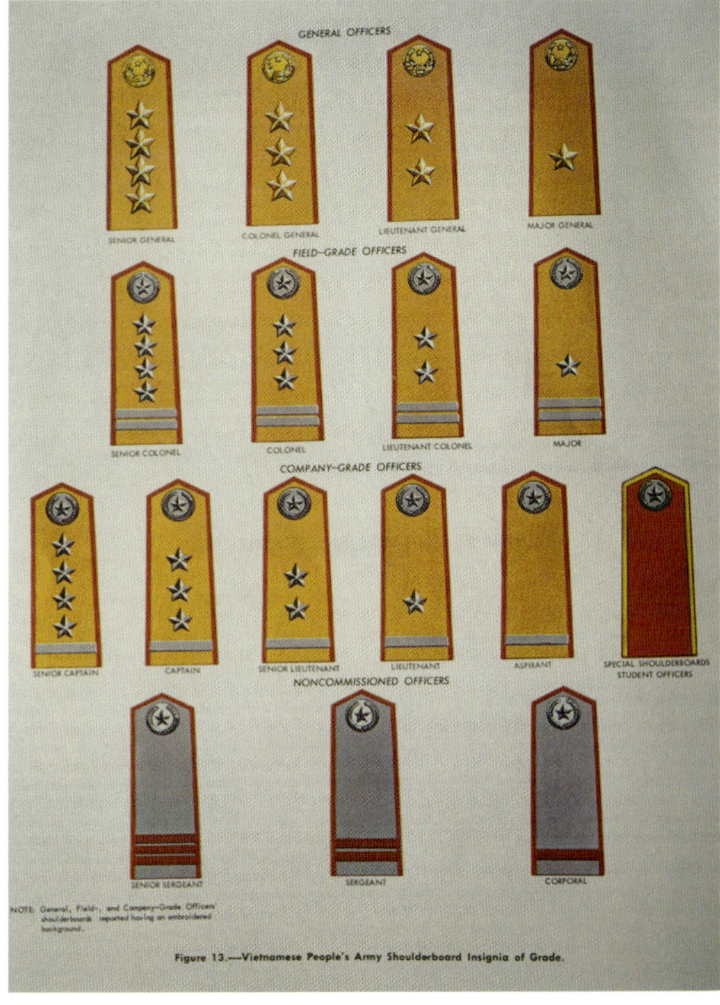

NCOs of the PAVN, courtesy " handbook nr 30.55 Sino-Soviet ground forces Asian members HQ dept of the army Washington DC 25."

Republic of Vietnam 1949-1954

The first camouflage, for airborne troops, was very similar to the pattern used by the British in World War II and worn by the French army from 1946 to 1950 in the Indochina war. The second pattern was similar to the U.S. army leaf pattern and was also reserved for airborne troops.

At the same time, the Republican Army of Vietnam (RAVN) police were issued special camouflage uniforms in the so-called "cloud" pattern. This refers to the existing U.S. pattern used for reversible helmet covers with green and brown "clouds –vineyard leaves."

In 1965 the RAVN was wearing jackets in vineyard leaf pattern for a short time. This pattern was later modified and used by South Korea for helmet covers.[1]

In 1968 the South Vietnamese army adopted a special tigerstripe camouflage pattern, until then only used by the U.S. army Special Forces. This pattern was very similar to the French lizard pattern of 1954. So, both the U.S. and RAVN Special Forces wore this camouflage. Ultimately many variants of the tigerstripe have been made.[2]

The rank insignia of the RAVN were the same as the ones used by the French army until 1955:

In 1955 Ngo Dinh Diem ordered the troops to rip off their French insignia and to burn them in front of the defeated French officers in order to humiliate them. The author was present at this sad and shameful meeting.

After 1955 the rank insignia were modified
Generals wore silver stars
Senior officers wore big silver flowers
NCOs wore silver or golden chevrons
Corporals wore yellow chevrons

1960 South Vietnamese airborne pattern, courtesy Military Illustrated, London.

1960 South Vietnamese RAVN paratroopers pattern similar to the U.S. woodland pattern, courtesy "World militaria, Leo Karlin USA Texas."

Close-up of the RAVN cloud pattern.

RAVN military police cloud pattern.

Paratroopers of the RAVN with camouflage similar to the U.S. leaf pattern, but with a dominant green color.

1965 vineyards leaf pattern.

1965 South Vietnamese paratrooper. RR

Second type of tigerstripe pattern, courtesy "World militaria, Leo Karlin USA Texas."

First type of tigerstripe pattern. AC

Third type of tigerstripe pattern. AC

Officers' rank insignia and cap badges.

NCOs rank insignia and paratroopers badges.

Camouflage distributed by the U.S. army to mountain tribes who revolted against the Vietcong, courtesy "National Geographic magazine January 1965 p 38 – 64."

Camouflage and insignia of soldiers of the RAVN, courtesy Amilitaria magazine, Brussels Belgium - drawing P. Courcelles.

Camouflage and unit badges, 9 is a mountain camouflage, courtesy Amilitaria magazine, Brussels Belgium - drawing P. Courcelles.

1
KAZAK.
UZBEK
KASPIAN SEA
TURKM.
5
4
3
2
GEORG.
AZER.
ARM.
RUSSIA
KAZAKHSTAN
KASPIAN SEA
ARAL
AZERB.
UZBEK.
KIRG.
TURKM.
TADJIK.
IRAN
AFGHA.
INDIA

2

Central Asia and the Caucasus Region

Afghanistan

The first camouflaged uniforms were introduced in 1974 and were worn by the paratroopers of the Daoud army.

From 1974 on, the Afghan army under the pro-Communist leadership of president Najibullah was wearing Soviet camouflage patterns.

In 1986 a Bulgarian camouflage pattern with a clear brown background was issued to the Afghan paratroopers.

In 1988 anti-Communist guerillas under the leadership of commander Massoud used British DPM camouflage when engaged in fights against the Russians.

Under the Taliban regime all fighters supporting the government wore traditional clothing, rather than military uniforms. Camouflaged uniforms were a rare feature in the official army.

In 2001-2002 the northern alliance, supported by the U.S., defeated the Taliban and recaptured the country. The troops of the alliance wore a mixture of uniforms, many with Indonesian, South Korean, Russian, and older Chinese patterns. A larger number of troops were wearing Turkish-made camouflage uniforms. Financed by the U.S., the Turkish government provided the Northern Alliance with the necessary means to defeat the Taliban.

Rank insignia seem to have never been modified since the monarchy; only the cap badges changed over the years. This badge consists of a mosque surrounded by foliage during the monarchy of Zaher Shah (1963-1973), an eagle with spread wings surrounded by foliage during the 1973 republic, and finally a red star, corn ears, and an opened book during the communist period of Najibullah.

- The infantry wears green collar patches; the air force wears blue patches.
- Generals and senior officers wear red collar tabs with three corn ears.
- The air force wears special rank insignia: blue shoulder boards with a bar and little stripes for junior officers, two bars and stripes for senior officers and three bars and stripes for generals.

The first known camouflage of the Afghan army, courtesy "World militaria, Leo Karlin USA Texas."

Bulgarian summer pattern for Afghan paratroopers.

Close-up view of the Bulgarian pattern.

Commander Massoud, courtesy Y. Debay.

Close-up view of British DPM camo.

2001 pattern made in Indonesia, courtesy Y. Debay.

South Korean pattern, courtesy Y. Debay.

Turkish pattern, courtesy Y. Debay.

Turkish pattern with French officer on the left, courtesy Terre magazine France.

At left is a Lt. colonel with corn ears on the collar patch, courtesy "Afghanistan today," 1985.

Rank insignia of the Afghan army: Generals, Afghan shield and stars; Senior officers, crossed swords and stars; Junior officers, bars and stars; and NCOs wear chevrons. Courtesy F Steff collections.

Typical cap of the Afghan army during the communist period.

President Najibullah at a parade.

Air force soldiers on parade.

Typical dress of an Afghan soldier. RR

Army and air force rank insignia, courtesy Mr. Holzel.

Plate with flags 1970 – 2002 and insignia.
1 1973 and 2002 flag.
2 Taliban flag.
3 Communist flag.
4 Republican eagle.
5 Republican eagle.
6 HQ collar tab.
7 – 10 Insignia

Armenia

The camouflage uniforms of the Armenian army in 2002 are the same as the Russian ones. Rank insignia are also similar to the Russian, except for generals. They wear the national emblem of Armenia on their hats: a shield with an eagle and a lion.

Lower rank forage caps have a similar shield surrounded by foliage and topped by a cockade with the national colors: blue, white, and red in three concentric circles.

Shoulder boards are edged by red piping for the army, blue piping for the air force, and a green one for border troops.

Armenia has had an independent army since 1991.

Russian autumn camo.

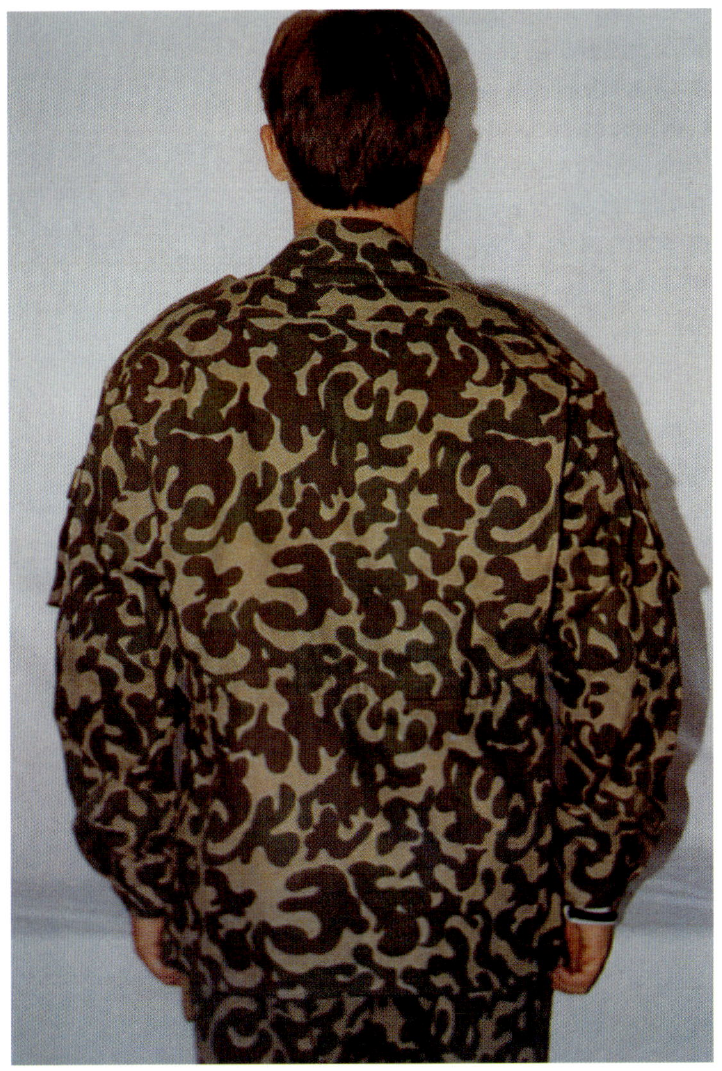

Common camouflage suit for Georgia and Armenia 2002. There is no information known about this pattern, courtesy Dennis Desmond.

General badge and camo purpose.

Insignia of the Armenian army:
1 cap badges
2 rank insignia of junior officers, senior officers and generals.

Cap badge of an Armenian officer, courtesy Rudolf Hölzel.

Azerbaijan

Azerbaijan is one of the former Soviet countries that quickly abandoned the Russian insignia and camouflage patterns. The pattern of their present camouflage is new but very similar to the U.S. leaf pattern, a design which is widely spread throughout many armies of the world (Spain, Italy, Turkey, Slovenia...).

The rank insignia are completely different from the Russian ones: eight-pointed stars (1 to 4) for junior officers on a very trimmed design for parade purposes, and 1 to 4 golden eight-pointed stars on the battle dress; senior officers wear 1 to 3 eight-pointed stars with foliage underneath, while generals wear large eight-pointed stars. The cap badge represents a circle with an eight-pointed star and red flames, encircled by a foliage wreath. On the forage cap the badge is far more simple: a star, crescent, and foliage. NCOs, however, wear the same rank insignia as in the former Russian army.

Azeri soldier with the new camouflage pattern, similar to the U.S. M65 design courtesy Y. Debay.

Close-up of the Azerbaijan pattern with justice badge.

CH2/25

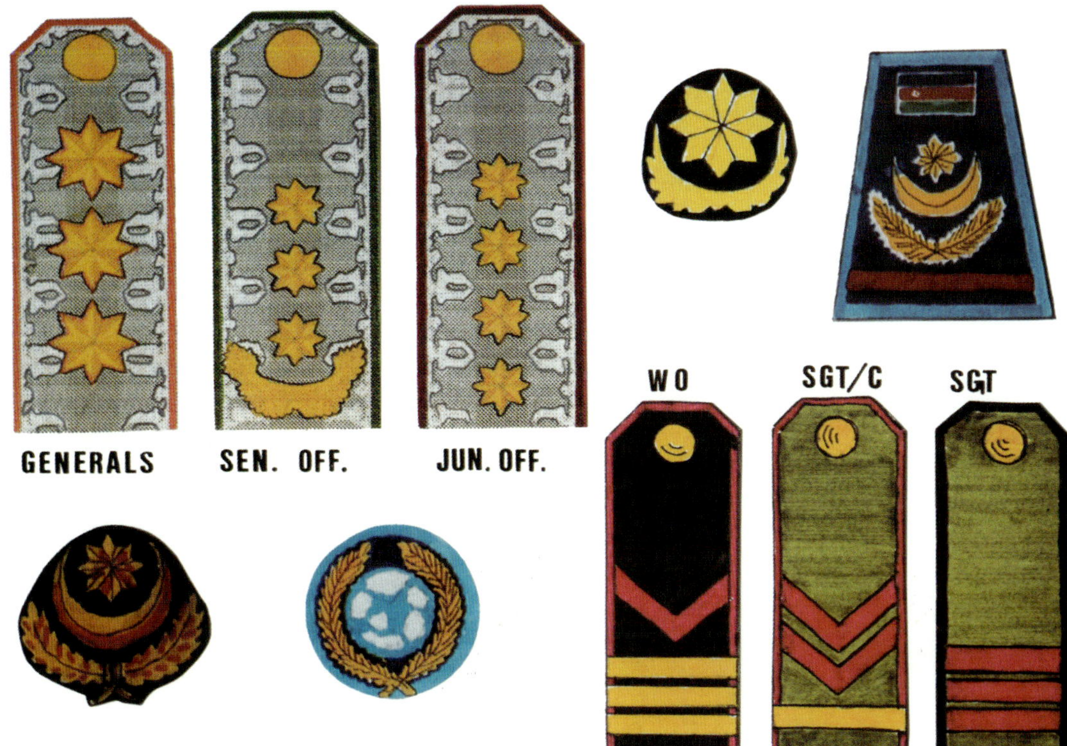

Rank insignia of Azerbaijan:
1st line cap and arm badges NCOs
2nd line collar and cap badges
3rd line parade shoulder boards of all officers' ranks
Rank insignia of Azeri army, parade shoulder boards; officers, NCOs, and WO shoulder boards cap badges and arm insignia, courtesy A. Fichiers army.

Georgia

The Georgian army has also chosen a pattern different from the former Russian army. The Georgian pattern has an amoeba light green to violet network on an olive drab background. In one of the photos one can see a Georgian soldier wearing a blue beret, trained by a Greek instructor.

The rank insignia are the same as the Russian ones, only this time with seven-pointed stars, and they are placed in a more longitudinal way.

NCOs wear new insignia; chevrons that are based upon the new Russian rank system. Specialty badges are worn on the collar tabs.

Georgian camouflage pattern, courtesy Y. Debay.

A Georgian major with the Russian shoulder boards, but with the seven-pointed stars, courtesy R. Holzel.

A captain of the Georgian army with 4 stars. Notice the new cap badge, courtesy Rudolf Hölzel.

A NCO with rank chevrons of a senior sergeant.

Plate with rank insignia of the Georgian army. Shoulder boards of 1st lieutenant, major, captain, and general. The seven-pointed star is the symbol of Georgia (St George and the lance) Arm shields consist of two lions and a sword and special Georgian character writings. Arm badge for ABKASY MVD. Courtesy G. Plotkin, Moscow.

Iran

In 1979 Shah Pahlevi left Tehran and went into exile in Egypt. At that time the Iranian army used two different camouflage patterns: the vertical French "lizard" pattern and a desert pattern. When the new Islamic government of Ayatollah Khomeini went to war against Iraq in 1980 these patterns were still in use. During the eight years of the war a new type of warrior emerged. Groups of Islamic soldiers who were ready to die for Allah like Kamikaze soldiers, named "Pasdarans," wore a very curious camouflage pattern. This design was made of red, green, and black ragged drawings on a clear brown background. These Pasdarans often were still very young and very fanatic. The camouflage they wore was not very effective and mainly had an encouraging purpose.

The war ended without a clear victory on either side. After the war the camouflage patterns changed, and many existing patterns from other armies were adopted.

The Iranian army never modified her rank insignia, thus keeping those used by the former army of Shah Pahlevi. Only the insignia for generals changed by order of the new government: the royal crown was replaced by an Islamic symbol.

Senior officers wear 1 to 3 large pips with the name of Allah in Persian characters.

Junior officers wear 1 to 3 five-pointed stars.

NCOs wear chevrons as do WOs and these chevrons are very similar to the ones used by the U.S. army.

The cap insignia for generals is an Islamic shield with an arm holding a machine gun.

Soldiers at the parade for the departure of Shah Pahlevi Iran 1979. RR

Cadet of the Iranian army.

Close-up view of the 1970-1980 pattern.

Desert pattern of the Iranian army 1980. RR

Close-up view of the 1980 Iranian desert pattern.

Green pattern for the Iranian army 1980.

Close-up view of the camouflage pattern.

A new camouflage pattern emerged in 1988. RR

Close-up view of the new pattern.

Opposite: *A young Pasdaran in the typical camouflage suit carrying a picture of Khomeini. The inscription on his head says "There is only one God and Mohammed is his prophet." RR*

Plate with rank insignia and cap badges of the Iranian army.

General's visor cap with the typical Iranian symbol, courtesy Marc Landry.

Close-up view of the Russian pattern used in Kazakhstan.

Kazakhstan

In 1991 Kazakhstan gained its independence and Noursoultan Nazarbaev became president.

They adopted the former Russian camouflage patterns, but modified the rank insignia for officers. NCOs and lower ranks kept the Russian insignia.

Officers wear very decorated shoulder boards with one bar and 1 to 3 stars for junior officers, two bars and 1 to 3 stars for senior officers, and an eagle with spread wings for generals.

The bars used are red for the army, blue for air forces, and gold for parade uniforms.

The cap badges are the shield of Kazakhstan or a single cockade Russian style for forage caps.

A Kazakh captain in parade uniform, courtesy Rudolf Hölzel.

Captain of the air force, courtesy GL Plotkin Moscow Russia.

A Kazakh lieutenant colonel, note the "KZ" at the collar and the fine decoration of the shoulder boards, courtesy Rudolf Hölzel.

Kazakh soldiers on parade wearing the Russian camouflage pattern 2002. RR

Rank insignia and cap badges of the army of Kazakhstan.

Arm badges of the Kazakh army.

Arm badges and cap badges of the army of Kazakhstan.

General and officers of Kazakhstan together with their president.

Kyrgyzstan

Kyrgyzstan became independent from the Soviet Union in 1991. They use the same camouflage patterns as the Russian army in 2002.

The rank insignia they use are also the same as the ones used by the Russian army.

The symbol of Kyrgyzstan, worn as a cockade of the Russian type, is an eagle and a sun over the mountains. The shoulder boards have a red piping for the army and blue for the air force.

Kyrgyzs 2002 camouflage pattern.

Air force lieutenant colonel with a forage cap, courtesy Rudolf Hölzel.

Kyrgyzs rank insignia, only the buttons have been changed and wear the Kyrgyzs symbol.

A Kyrgyzs major of the army, note the special badge with the Kyrgyzs flag.

Mongolia

Mongolia gained independence in 1945. The camouflage patterns they use are very much influenced by the Russian designs. The rank insignia, however, have all the characteristics of Asian armies. Most rank insignia represent very old traditional drawings in a truly decorative way.

The cap badge shows traditional Mongolian symbols in a cockade, similar to Russian ones. Mongolian shoulder boards are mostly slip-on models.

Mongolian camouflage pattern of Chinese origin. PLA Pictorial 2000, Bejing.

Mongolian officers (a colonel and a captain) with characteristic slip-on shoulder boards. Note the unit arm badge, courtesy Rudolf Hölzel.

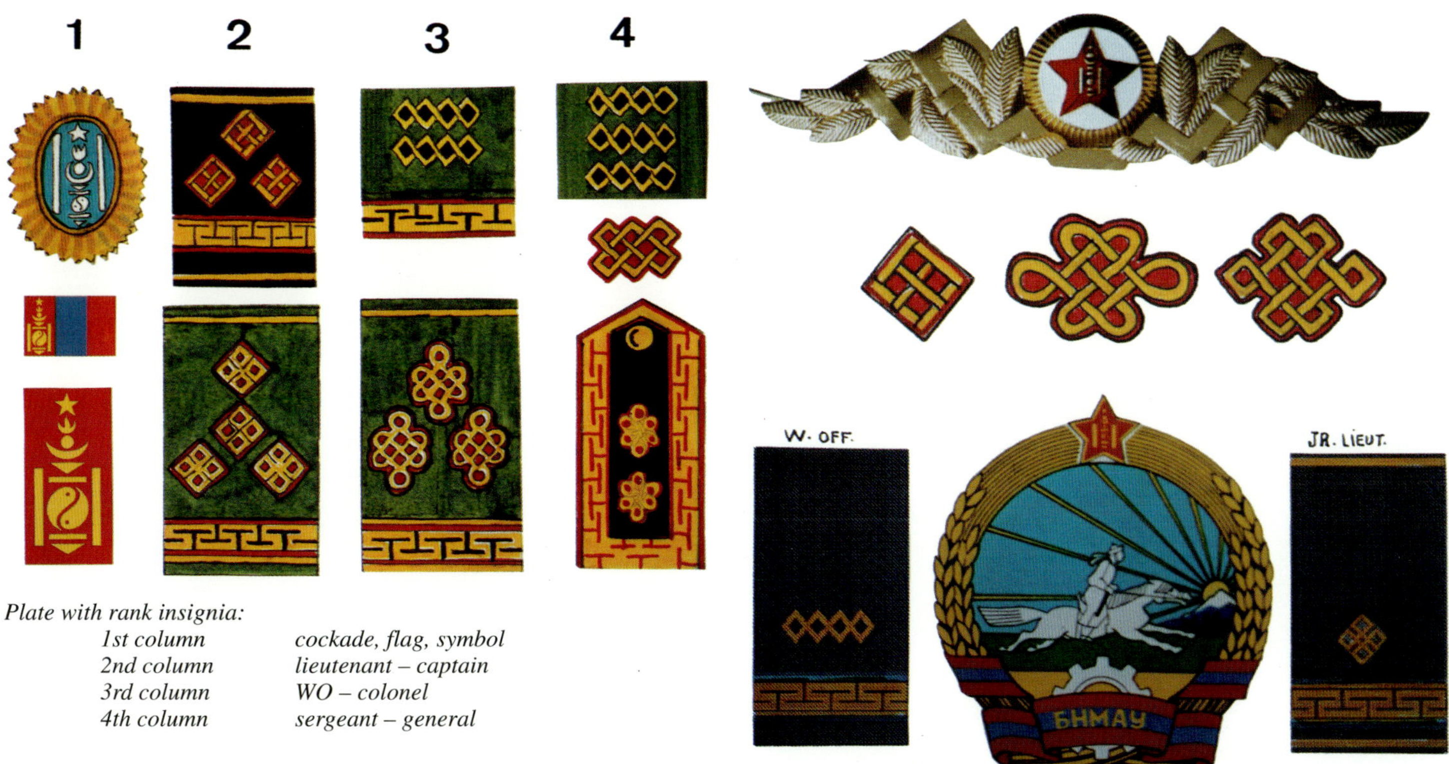

Plate with rank insignia:

1st column	*cockade, flag, symbol*
2nd column	*lieutenant – captain*
3rd column	*WO – colonel*
4th column	*sergeant – general*

Detail of drawings for junior officers and a senior officer's Badge of Mongolia in 1950. Left: master sergeant, right: lieutenant.

Uzbekistan

Independent since 1991, the army of Uzbekistan wears a camouflage pattern made in Russia, but with a special design for its own.

The rank insignia are the same as the Russian 2002 rank insignia with only one difference: the stars are eight-pointed. The officer's cap badge is a phoenix with spread wings, with a crescent and a star on a blue background. A wreath of foliage edged with the national colors encircles the phoenix in blue, white, and green.

Paratroopers wear the phoenix, a blue star with crescent, and a pair of wings over the national colors topped by a parachute. The shoulder boards have colored piping: red for the army, blue for the air force.

A colonel of Uzbekistan with the special pattern for Uzbekistan and 3 eight-pointed stars on his shoulder board. RR

Cap badge of Uzbeki paratroopers and special badge for color berets, courtesy Rudolf Hölzel.

Two majors of Uzbekistan, courtesy Rudolf Hölzel.

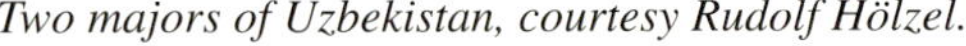

Badges of Uzbeki paratroopers with beret cap badge, unit badge, and flag and arm badge, courtesy G. Plotkin, Moscow.

Rank insignia of Uzbekistan.
1st line sergeant, WO, second captain, lieutenant colonel, air force colonel.
2nd line first captain, unit badge, general. Note the eight-pointed stars for all officers.

Russian-made camo pattern designed for Uzbekistan. RR

Detail of the officers' cap insignia.

Pakistan

The army of Pakistan created its first camouflage uniform in 1970. It was a very characteristic pattern that was sold to many African and Middle Eastern armies. It seems that two types have been manufactured: one in dark green and brown drawings in 1970; and another in green khaki and brown drawings in 1980. Two other patterns have been created for UNO operations IFOR and KFOR in Bosnia and Kosovo. At present time, certain elite units like the commandos of the Pakistani army are wearing the British DPM pattern.

Rank insignia of the Pakistani army are similar to the British insignia, only the pips have been modified and a crescent and star replace the crown.

Generals wear an insignia with crossed swords and a baton; NCOs wear chevrons. The air force has nearly the same rank insignia as the British Royal Air Force.

Typical camouflage pattern of Pakistan, sold in 1980 to Ethiopia, Iraq, and Lebanon. RR

Modified colors of the 1980 pattern.

Close-up view of the Pakistani pattern.

The new Pakistani pattern in 1990.

Pakistani pattern worn by UNO forces during IFOR and KFOR in the nineties, courtesy Nicolas Peucelle, courtesy World militaria, Leo Karlin USA Texas.

General of the air force and an admiral of Pakistan. RR

British DPM pattern worn by elite troops.

Plate with Pakistani rank insignia, courtesy Steff.

Regimental badges and unit insignia of Pakistan.

Tajikistan

Tajikistan gained independence from the Soviet Union in 1991. The army has kept using the Russian rank insignia until today. The camouflage patterns used seem to be of Turkish origin (also worn by Afghanistan and Iraq). Only the national emblem has changed, and now it shows a crown topped by seven stars. This symbol also occurs in the national flag. On the military uniforms, this emblem has replaced the Russian cockade.

Above:*Turkish camouflage used by the army of Tajikistan, courtesy Leo Karlin.* Right: *Tajikistani colonel wearing Russian rank insignia and still with a communist cockade. RR*

Close-up view of this pattern.

Arm badges of the Tajikistani army, courtesy G. Plotkin, Moscow.

Rank insignia of the army of Tajikistan, courtesy G. Plotkin, Moscow.

Turkmen lieutenant senior grade, courtesy Rudolf Hölzel.

Turkmenistan

Turkmenistan gained independence from the Soviet Union in 1991. The army has kept using the Russian rank insignia and camouflage patterns until today.

The cockade they use consists of five silver stars on a green background. An old badge used in 1943-1944 displays a horse in a circle of corn ears with seven white flowers. The arm badge has an inscription in Roman characters.

Cap badge of a Turkmen officer, courtesy Rudolf Hölzel.

Shoulder boards of a captain and a lieutenant (two degrees of Russian origin).

Arm badges and rank insignia on shoulder boards of the Turkmen army, courtesy GL Plotkin.

1st line Bahrain, UAE, Iraq, Israel
2nd line Jordan, Kuwait, Lebanon, Oman
3rd line Palestine, Qatar, Saudi Arabia
4th line Syria, Egypt, Yemen

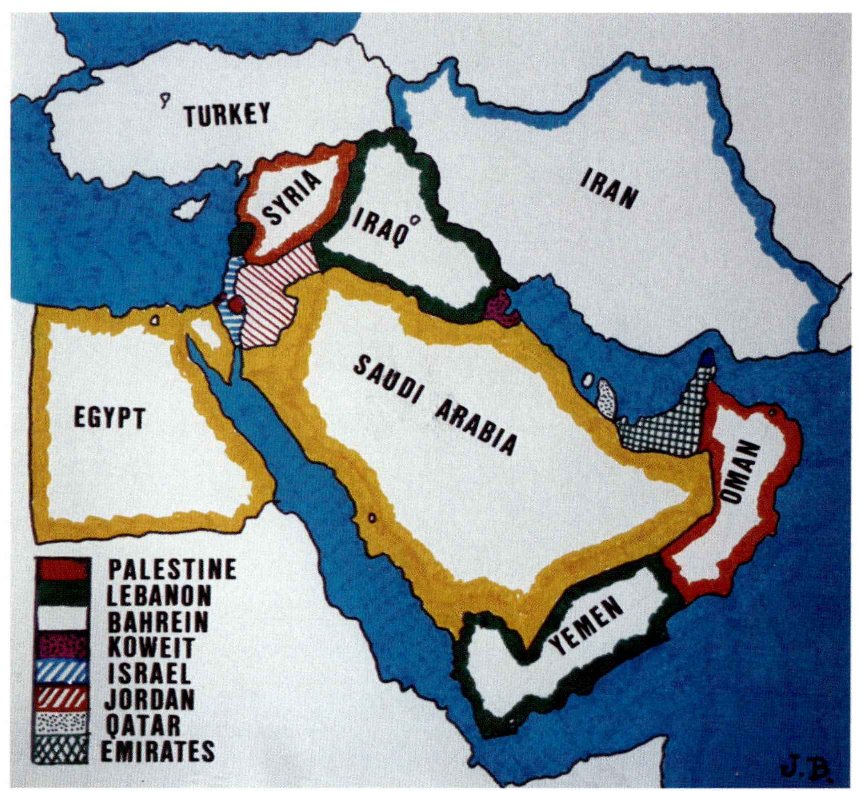

3

Middle East

Bahrain

Bahrain has been an independent nation since 1971. The national insignia is a red and white shield with a royal crown encircled by red and white foliage. Recently the crown was removed from the insignia.

The camouflage pattern is a sort of "tiger stripe" design, but the colors are black and light and dark brown on a white background.

Earlier they used a desert camouflage in the British DPM pattern and also the U.S. army "chocolate chips" pattern.

Rank insignia are chevrons for NCOs, 1 to 3 eight-pointed stars for junior officers, and a crown and eight-pointed stars for senior officers. Generals wear two crossed swords and a star or a crown.

General insignia of the Middle Eastern armies, courtesy M. Landry collection.

Camouflage pattern of the army of Bahrain, courtesy Leo Karlin.

British desert DPM pattern used by Bahrain.

Bahrain soldiers in the Gulf War against Iraq. RR

Rank insignia of the army of Bahrain: a pilot badge and visor cap insignia.

Egypt

The Egyptian army has modified all its insignia after the departure of King Farouk in 1952. An eagle carrying a red, white, and black shield has replaced the crown in the insignia.

The first camouflage uniforms were created before the first war against Israel in 1956 (Suez crisis) and strongly resemble the German Waffen SS 1939 – 1945 zeltbahn camouflage pattern. These uniforms were reversible and had ochre and green spots on one side and yellow and brown spots on the other. The side with green spots was intended for rocky terrain, while the brown side was for the desert areas.

In 1973 two new camouflage patterns were introduced, among which was a curious one with large brown drawings used for quarter shelters or uniforms, and which was made of a very light material of poor quality.

In 1989 this pattern was modified: the brown drawings became ragged and had large spots between them. Later these spots were diminished and were shaped like small branches. This was the pattern used by the Egyptians during the Gulf War.

Today most Egyptian soldiers wear the Gulf War pattern or the M65 U.S. army pattern.

Rank insignia are 1 to 4 chevrons for NCOs, 1 to 3 stars for junior officers and an eagle and stars for senior officers. Generals wear crossed swords and stars.

The collar tabs of senior officers have golden lotus flowers on them; the cap badge also has a lotus flower in it. The national shield on the headgear has an eagle with lotus crown.

Other ranks' headgear only displays the eagle.

Paratroopers wear a silver eagle.

Egyptian paratroopers wearing the ochre rock camouflage pattern in 1956.

Close-up view of this pattern.

Desert side of the Egyptian camouflage.

Close-up view of the 1973 ochre rock pattern.

Special camouflage pattern of the Egyptian army in 1973, used for tents and uniforms.

The new Gulf War pattern from 1989-1990: brown, black, and large green spots. Pattern was abandoned in 1990. RR

Pattern similar to the U.S. M65 pattern used in 1992 by the Egyptian army, courtesy Leo Karlin.

Opposite: *Ochre rock side of the 1956 quarter shelter (zeltbahn) very similar to the German Waffen-SS oak leaf pattern of 1939-1945.*

Modified 1990 pattern with thin drawings in stead of large spots.

Above left: *Egyptian soldiers during the Gulf War in 1991 wearing the 1956 pattern, courtesy Y. Debay.* Left: *A general of the Egyptian army ECPA. RR*

Cap and rank insignia of the Egyptian army, courtesy M. Landry collection.

Collar tabs and unit shields for Egyptian officers.

Generals of the Egyptian army, navy, and air force. RR

The 1989-1990 camouflage suit with insignia for a captain of the commandos, courtesy Leo Karlin.

United Arab Emirates

In 1971 seven countries joined forces and are now called the United Arab Emirates (UAE). These countries were: Adman; Abu Dabi; Dubai; Chardja; Um el Kaywayn; Ras al Khayma; and Fudjayra. Camouflage patterns differed according to the country they came from. Many were of British origin or based upon U.S. desert patterns. After the Gulf War many new desert camouflage uniforms have been created in the region, many of which were made in Arab countries.

The rank insignia of the UAE are similar to the British: chevrons for NCOs, but the crown has been replaced by a phoenix topped by a star. Junior officers wear 1 to 3 golden stars, and senior officers wear a phoenix and 1 to 3 golden stars. Generals wear crossed swords and a baton with stars. On the shoulder boards one encounters the name of each emirate, written in Arabic.

The shield of the emirates is an eagle with an Arab ship called "felouk," underscored by the inscription: "United Arab Emirates." Each emirate has its own flag, in which the red color is dominant.

Close combat between two soldiers wearing a pattern made in Arab countries. RR

Special and rare camouflage with "long brown fingers" and branches. RR

Variant of U.S. "chocolate chips" for a sergeant of the UAE.

Rank insignia of UAE.

British DPM worn by UAE soldiers 1985. RR

A general of the army of the UAE. RR

Parade uniform for special air forces of the UAE, courtesy Dr. Landry.

Iraq

At the beginning of the Iraq-Iran war, which lasted 8 years (1982 to 1990), Saddam Husseins' armies wore at least five different camouflage patterns. The first one was inspired by the German RDA patterns: ragged brown leaves with dark blue and green variations, mainly worn by paratroopers. The other designs are similar to the U.S. M65 pattern and to the Belgian 1953 "brush" pattern. Another was even similar to the Waffen-SS oak leaf pattern, but with different colors. The French lizard pattern was also encountered, and of course the British DPM desert pattern that was sold to Iraq in 1980.

This forced Her Majesty's army to modify its own camouflage patterns during the Gulf War in 1991 in order not to confuse friendly troops with an enemy wearing the same camouflage.

Finally, a curious uniform was manufactured for the political Bath party and mainly worn by guards and child-soldiers. This uniform had a pattern composed of different drawings: palm trees and country maps of the Middle East!

The rank insignia of the Iraqi army are similar to the British ones. In this army the traditional "pips" are replaced by stars, the crown has been replaced by the Iraqi eagle holding a shield with 3 green stars and a line of the Koran. NCOs wear long diagonal black bands (1 to 4).

Iraqi paratroopers pattern, similar to the RDA camouflage.

Close-up view of the paratrooper pattern.

Speckled pattern similar to German Waffen-SS oak leave pattern, courtesy Leo Karlin.

Left British DPM desert pattern, right "Brush" pattern similar to Belgian camouflage.

Close-up view of "brush" pattern, courtesy Leo Karlin.

"Popular forces" camouflage similar to U.S. M65 pattern, courtesy Leo Karlin.

Iraqi pilot prisoner of the Iranian army, 1986.

Iraqi soldiers wearing the French lizard pattern and the British DPM pattern. RR

Close-up view of the French lizard pattern, courtesy Leo Karlin.

Young girl of the Bath party of Saddam Hussein. RR

Plate with rank insignia and cap badges of the Iraqi army.

Israel

In 1956 the army of Israel wore one type of camouflage of French origin during the war against Egypt. From 1957 to 1998 the Israeli army was probably the only regular army in the world that did not wear a camouflage pattern. The soldiers all wear olive drab uniforms. The only camouflage feature they wear is the helmet cover. This has three colors: green, violet, and brown. Snipers supposedly also wear uniforms in this pattern, and maybe one day it can become the Israeli pattern, but so far the helmet cover is the only garment in camouflage that is actually worn.

Rank insignia are fig tree leaves (1 to 3) for senior officers, bars of olive tree branches (1 to 3) for junior officers. Generals wear crossed olive tree branches and a sword. Warrant officers wear 1 to 3 chevrons topped by a star.

French lizard pattern used by the Israeli army during the war of 1956.

This camouflage is not a suit but a sort of camouflage network, courtesy Raids magazine.

A sniper wearing his camo netting, courtesy Raids magazine.

Rank insignia of the Israeli army with cap badges and slip-on shoulder boards.

Recently issued new rank insignia for warrant officers.

Rank badges and beret insignia, courtesy Landry.

A paratrooper general of the Israeli army. RR

Cap badges for artillery, air force, army, armored cars, supplies, and technicians.

Jordan

The Jordanian army has long been commanded by the famous British general Glubb Pasha, therefore it was very much influenced by the British army uniforms and insignia.

In the 1980s the army wore a British light Denison smock. At present time it wears a camouflage similar to the U.S. M65 pattern.

The Jordanian police is wearing a [something missing here?] with a blue British DPM camouflage pattern.

Rank insignia are very similar to the British ones but again pips are replaced, this time by seven-pointed stars. NCOs wear chevrons, officers have a red collar tab with a golden lace and button. A captain wears 3 stars, a colonel a crown and 2 stars a general wears crossed swords and stars.

British pattern Denison smock for the Jordanian army, courtesy Leo Karlin.

1980 Jordanian pattern, courtesy Leo Karlin.

Jordanian police.

King Hussein talking to his soldiers. RR

Air force generals' cap.

The young king, then a colonel of the Jordanian army. RR

Plate with rank insignia and cap badges of the Jordanian army.

Kuwait

The army of Kuwait is wearing a British-made camouflage desert pattern. After the Gulf War against Iraq the U.S. and the UK have become significant allies and major providers of army clothing and equipment.

Besides the British-made uniform a variation – probably made in the region – has also been distributed to the troops.

Rank insignia are similar to the British insignia: stars have replaced the pips and the crown is replaced by the national symbol of Kuwait.

NCOs wear chevrons, junior officers 1 to 3 golden stars, senior officers the symbol of Kuwait and 1 to 3 stars and generals wear crossed swords and stars.

In 2002 the national symbol of Kuwait has been modified and was replaced by a crown.

Kuwaiti army general (left) and a major. RR

Kuwaiti soldier with two sorts desert pattern uniforms, courtesy Y. Debay.

Colonel in British desert DPM, courtesy Y. Debay.

Kuwaiti general and brigadier of the army. RR

Rank insignia and cap badges.

Lebanon

On the outskirts of WWII Lebanon became an independent state and started to develop its own army.

The camouflage patterns worn by this army were often modified.

The first pattern was worn at the beginning of the sixties and was a copy of an existing Egyptian pattern with reversible sand areas (see the Egyptian chapter)

In 1975-1977 a new camouflage design appeared. It was of Pakistani origin and was worn until 1980 when the war against Syria raged, which ended with a UN intervention. During the Israeli occupation and the emerging of many Christian militia troops, the official camouflage patterns changed again: a gray uniform for police and a M81 U.S. woodland pattern for the army. The latter was used until 1986.

Today the Lebanese army wears a sort of U.S. woodland copy; the police, however, still wears their gray uniforms.

Rank insignia are red chevrons for corporals and golden ones for NCOs. Warrant officers wear large five-pointed stars (one big and one little), junior officers wear 1 to 3 stars, and senior officers wear a star circled by a wreath of leaves topped by one or two stars. Generals wear a crossed stick and sword as insignia and they also have a special cap badge where 3 symbols are gathered: swords an anchor and wings.

In 2002 the stars have been modified with a cedar of Lebanon in the center.

The first camouflage pattern of the Lebanese army courtesy Leo Karlin.

Reversed side of the Egyptian pattern copy: rocks with ochre areas, courtesy Leo Karlin.

Pakistani pattern in the Lebanese army.

Close-up view of the gray pattern with British DPM designs.

Lebanese police with gray pattern. RR

General of the Army with U.S. M81 woodland camo. RR

Plate with rank insignia of the Lebanese army. AC

Generals' cap badge, courtesy Landry.

Lebanese shoulder board slip-ons for colonel and major with cap badges.

Oman

The army of the Red Sea sultanate of Oman wears a light material uniform in British DPM pattern with a very clear green background.

The British ones again inspired the design of the rank insignia, this time with a special crown.

NCOs wear chevrons, warrant officers wear leaves and a crown on the cuffs and officers wear a crown and stars.

The national symbol of Oman consists of Arab swords and a belt with the characteristic dagger.

Plate with rank insignia of the army of Oman, courtesy Steff collections.

Pilot and cap badge of the air force of Oman. The crown indicates the rank of major, courtesy Steff collections.

The Sultan of Oman with the clear DPM pattern. RR

Close-up view of the Oman camouflage pattern, courtesy Leo Karlin.

Palestine

Since 1950 the Palestinians have worn many different camouflaged uniforms, most of them bought of leftover stocks from other countries. The first pattern used by Palestinians came from South Korea. Later Iraqi suits emerged and many militia troops started using them. Now all sorts of patterns are used: Russian; American; and even Thai! Many of them are locally produced copies. Palestinian children often wear locally made camouflage garments.

South Korean camouflage pattern worn by Palestinians 1955- 1960. RR

Above: *Close-up view of the South Korean pattern.* Above right: *Pattern worn by children. RR*

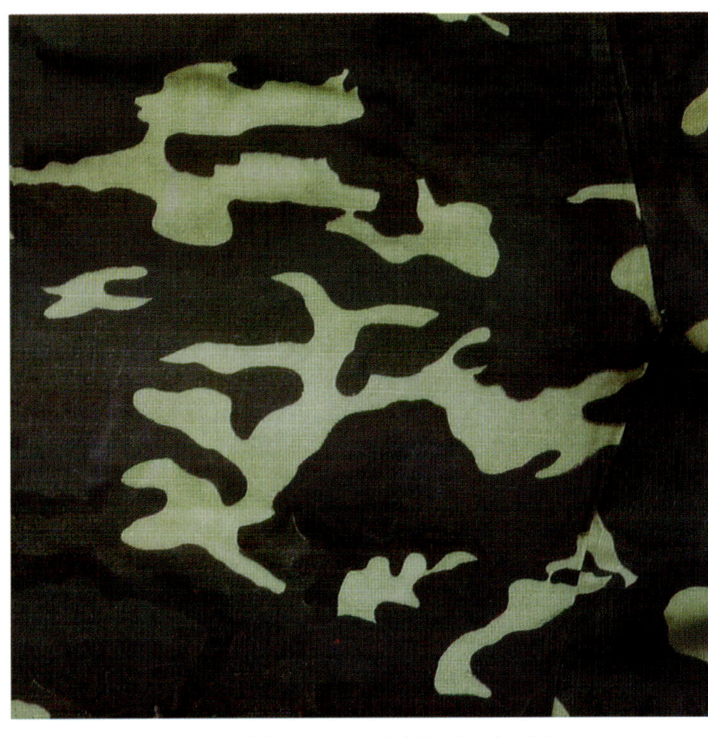

Above: *Close-up view of Thai pattern.* Right: *Iraqi origin pattern.*

Syrian origin camouflage, courtesy Leo Karlin.

Unknown origin worn by Palestinians in 2002.

Close-up view of Palestinian police pattern.

Plate with Palestinian rank insignia.

Qatar

This small country near the Persian Gulf gained independence in 1971. The camouflage uniforms used by its army have the British desert DPM pattern and a newer pattern developed in 2001. This latest pattern has large dark brown spots and stone shadows (like the U.S. desert pattern "chocolate chips") on a yellow sand background.

The rank insignia are very similar to the British ones.
NCOs wear golden chevrons.
Junior officers wear "pips" and senior officers "pips" and a crown.

British desert DPM for Qatar.

Close-up view of the Qatar pattern.

Color variant.

Rank insignia for NCOs and officers with their cap badge.

Insignia of the army of Qatar and the new 2001 pilot wings.

Saudi Arabia

After the Gulf War the army of Saudi Arabia has become one of the most important and best-equipped armies of the Middle East. In the '80s the French manufacturer "Texunion" developed a special camouflage pattern for the Saudis, which was used until 1987. Just before the Gulf War the Saudi army used the British DPM camouflage, though after the war the U.S. desert patterns were introduced. At first the army was equipped with the U.S. desert "chocolate chips" pattern, but later, in 1992, they used a newer camouflage design.

Saudi police units were equipped with a British pattern that was made with dominant gray and blue colors. This special camouflage was sold to many Arab countries.

The rank insignia are similar to the British insignia: NCOs wear chevrons and bars, junior officers wear stars, senior officers wear a crown and stars and generals wear crossed swords and stars.

The cap badge is made of a palm tree, two Arab swords and a crown.

Every unit wears a shoulder tab with Arab characters.

British DPM variant for the Saudi army, courtesy Leo Karlin.

Close-up view of French pattern.

Police camouflage of British origin, courtesy Leo Karlin.

French pattern especially made for Saudi Arabia.

U.S. desert pattern used by the Saudis in 1990.

New U.S. desert pattern for the Saudis after the Gulf war in 1992.

General and officers of Saudi Arabia ECPA.

Rank insignia and cap badges, courtesy M. Landry & Steff.

Shoulder tabs of paratroopers, Special Forces, and commandos.

At the right General of Saudi Arabia, at the left Jordanian air force general, courtesy M. Landry.

Syria

Of all Middle Eastern countries, Syria certainly is the one that has used the most camouflage patterns for its army since 1959.

First they used a reversible suit; on one side it was very similar to the British DPM pattern, but then with black and khaki drawings, on the other side the camouflage was similar to the British Denison Smock pattern.

The second pattern was very similar to the French lizard pattern, but with vertical stripes. The Saïka division mainly used this.

The third pattern seems to be of East German origin and emerged in 1970. It had blue, brown, and green oak leaves.

Later several units of the Syrian army wore the famous "pink panther" pattern. It was based upon a similar French design, used by French UN troops while guarding facilities in Lebanon. The Syrians modified the outlook a little bit by adding more pink and orange colors.

Finally, Syrian commandos were equipped with a camouflage similar to the U.S. M65 pattern with clear green drawings.

The rank insignia are red chevrons for corporals, golden chevrons for NCOs and 1 to 3 stars on a green or black arm shield for warrant officers. The cap badge is an eagle with a black and white shield and two green stars.

Before 1990, this eagle was also worn on the shoulder boards under the stars. Today the eagle can be worn over or under the stars, depending the unit that wears it.

Generals wear the eagle on the shoulder boards and have stars and crossed swords under it.

First reversible pattern, similar to the British DPM pattern, courtesy Leo Karlin.

Reversed side with Denison Smock pattern.

Saïka division pattern, colonel of the air force, courtesy Leo Karlin.

East German pattern. RR

The famous " pink panther " pattern. RR

Syrian soldiers in Lebanon. RR

Syrian lieutenant colonel with U.S. M65 pattern.

Syrian soldiers in the gulf War. RR

Syrian colonel with green collar tabs, courtesy M. Landry.

Syrian colonel with green background shoulder boards.

President Assad with generals' shoulder boards. RR

Plate with NCO and WO rank insignia.

Shoulder boards of a captain and a colonel (in 2002, the eagle is above the stars) cap badge eagle. Paratroopers and commando badges and pilot wings.

Yemen

North Yemen became independent of the Ottoman Empire in 1918. The British, who had set up a protectorate area around the southern port of Aden in the 19th century, withdrew in 1967 from what became South Yemen. Three years later, the southern government adopted a Marxist orientation. The massive exodus of hundreds of thousands of Yemenis from the south to the north contributed to two decades of hostility between the states. The two countries were formally unified as the Republic of Yemen in 1990.

The army of Yemen uses a reversible Egyptian camouflage pattern. On one side it has a typical desert pattern, and on the reverse has an ochre background with green and blue ragged drawings.

Like many other Arab countries, Yemen has a special camouflage uniform for its police forces. This uniform has long vertical stripes in blue color variations, a bit similar to the French camouflage pattern of 1954-1956.

The rank insignia for NCOs are chevrons, junior officers have 1 to 3 golden stars, and senior officers wear a shield and 1 or 2 stars. The cap badge consists of a shield on which an eagle with spreaded wings and two flags are displayed. This eagle is the national symbol of Yemen. The air force wears the same insignia but in silver.

Egyptian pattern, desert side out.

Reverse side of Egyptian pattern.

Close-up view of this pattern.

Right: *Latest camouflage of Yemenite army.*

Above: *Blue police camo pattern.* Right: *Plate with rank insignia.*

Air force badges of Middle Eastern and African countries, courtesy Steff Collections.